FOR JASON SICKLES, WHO KNOWS SO
MUCH ABOUT BROTHERS, JOURNEYS, AND
WHAT MAKES FOR A GOOD STORY

—C. B.

TO ANDI SCHREIBER, FOR HER
FRIENDSHIP, SUPPORT, AND LOVE OF
ALL THINGS DANCE

—C. G.

THE Nutcracker COMES TO America

Millbrook Press
A division of Lerner Publishing Group, Inc.
241 First Avenue North
Minneapolis, MN 55401 USA

For reading levels and more information, look up this title at www.lernerbooks.com.

The photographs in this book are used with the permission of: Courtesy of the Museum of Performance
and Design (brothers on ladder), (vaudeville tour), (Lew Christensen in Filling Station), (Portrait of the
Christensen brothers); Wikimedia Commons (Nutcracker 1892); © Transcendental Graphics/Getty Images
(Leopold Stokowski); © Andrea Mohin/The New York Times/Redux (Urban Ballet).

Main body text set in Breughel Com 13/18. Typeface provided by Linotype AG.

Library of Congress Cataloging-in-Publication Data

Barton, Chris.
    The Nutcracker comes to America : how three ballet-loving brothers created a holiday tradition / by
  Chris Barton ; illustrations by Cathy Gendron.
      pages cm. — (Millbrook picture books)
    ISBN 978-1-4677-2151-6 (lb : alk. paper) — ISBN 978-1-4677-8848-9 (eb pdf)
    1. Nutcracker (Choreographic work)—History—Juvenile literature. 2. Christmas—United States—
  Juvenile literature. I. Title. II. Title: The Nutcracker comes to America.
  GV1790.N8B37 2015
    792.8'42—dc23   2014041289

Manufactured in the United States of America
1 — VI — 7/15/15

THE Nutcracker COMES TO America

HOW THREE BALLET-LOVING BROTHERS CREATED A HOLIDAY TRADITION

CHRIS BARTON
illustrated by CATHY GENDRON

Millbrook Press/Minneapolis

WHEN YOU THINK OF *THE NUTCRACKER,* YOU PROBABLY THINK OF THIS.

AND THIS.

AND MAYBE EVEN THIS.

YOU PROBABLY DON'T THINK OF THIS.

ONE HUNDRED YEARS AGO, hardly anyone in the United States
had ever heard of this old Russian ballet. So how did it become a holiday
tradition? Well, our story kicks off in a small Utah town in the early
1900s—and it's three brothers doing the kicking . . .

Whether William, Harold, and little brother Lew *liked* to dance didn't count for much. They were Christensens. And never mind how the rest of the local boys spent their Saturdays—dancing was what Christensens *did,* and they did it at the family's dancing school.

Then one day Uncle Pete waltzed into town with some ballerinas from Salt Lake City. And who would've thought?

William flipped for ballet dancers and ballet dancing alike—he believed it had the stuff to knock everybody's socks off.

Lew had loads of natural talent and was willing to let William teach him.

Hotheaded Harold opted for the army instead, and he marched off to military school. But after his grades plunged, Harold limped back home. He took over the family's dancing school while William and Lew shoved off from Utah with dreams of stages, spotlights, and showbiz.

Where to?

VAUDEVILLE!

And where's that?

Nowhere in particular, but the name applied to anywhere there was a curtain—Los Angeles, Chicago, New York City, and all points in between. With flash and dazzle borrowed from ballet, the brothers competed for applause with jugglers, clowns, magicians, and dancing elephants. They learned lots about showmanship along the way.

They quick-changed their names to something French- or Russian-
or Italian-sounding, because gasping audiences couldn't believe
that such acrobatic dancing could be done by Americans. William
eventually booted the second *i* out of his name, and he liked
"Willam" so much he went by it for the rest of his days.

Meanwhile, Harold—who had decided that Willam and Lew's style of dancing wasn't so bad after all—had been practicing, practicing, practicing, trying to catch up. After three years, he joined his brothers in New York. They all ate, drank, slept, dreamed, itched, scratched, inhaled, and exhaled ballet—that high-energy flash and dazzle as well as its graceful, storytelling side.

But before long, Willam left to get ballet going in Portland, Oregon. He needed something for his students to perform, and the conductor of the local youth symphony had a suggestion. This conductor, a Russian immigrant, had a hunch that bits and pieces of an old Christmas-themed ballet from back home would do the trick. The ballet was— you guessed it!—*The Nutcracker.*

Willam created a few dances—
choreography, it's called—to
go with music composed
decades earlier by Peter Ilyich
Tchaikovsky. Lots of the story
was left out, and this holiday
ballet was performed in the
middle of June, but the audience
must not have minded.

After the closing number, "Waltz of the Flowers," the two hundred or so dance students and young musicians got a standing ovation from the crowd. Willam would remember that response.

Meanwhile, back in New York, Lew was doing some choreography of his own. He came up with *Filling Station,* a ballet set in—who would've thought?—modern-day America! He made roles for truckers, a gangster, a state trooper, and a little girl who really needed to use the restroom. Harold helped out behind the scenes and also played a lost driver.

The first performance
of *Filling Station* was
compared to a cartoon
come to life onstage.

You would think that more terrific ballet must surely be on its way from this configuration of Christensens. But it was not to be.

Like a trio of dancers trying to share two spotlights, the brothers often wove in and out of one another's view. Harold paired up with Willam to teach in San Francisco while Lew—giving up what might have been the most glorious years of his dancing career—traded in his ballet shoes for army boots.

Lots of other dancers joined up with the military during World War II. That made things tough for Willam and Harold. And talent wasn't the only thing in short supply. Money for putting on productions was scarce too.

By 1944, to keep ballet alive in San Francisco, the Christensen brothers needed a hit. It had to be something that would appeal to adults and children alike.

While Willam was out and about, he noticed San Franciscans whistling the music of a popular composer—Tchaikovsky. That gave him an idea: Willam decided to have another go at *The Nutcracker*.

Not just bits and pieces of it, either. He and Harold were going to treat audiences to the whole shebang. So what if they hadn't actually seen the whole shebang themselves?

Willam and Harold huddled up with their friends George and Alexandra, who had danced in the whole show long ago in Russia.

Equipped with a better understanding of the story
and the characters and what all the dancing *meant*,
Willam built up the steps for a new production.

Harold built up the dancers so that they could do those steps. Patient, strict, and teasing all at once, and always standing so straight that his pants kept trying to slide down, Harold took special care in teaching the many young dancers taking part.

Lew couldn't be there himself, of course. But his wife, Gisella, was in the thick of things as the Sugar Plum Fairy.

Lots of other people pitched in too. They wanted to put on as big a show as they could on as small a budget as possible, because small was all they had.

Performers and their mothers helped make tutus. (One dancer got so involved that she had to be cut free from a sewing machine.)

An old red-velvet theater curtain got chopped up and used for costumes.

Many performers switched from role to role. In one scene, a soldier—in the next, a snowflake!

Now, folks in San Francisco were not in the habit of attending big shows during the holiday season. But it was on Christmas Eve, no less, that the Christensens and company put on the whole shebang.

And—who would've thought?—the War Memorial Opera House was packed. Aside from some troublesome wigs, *The Nutcracker* was a genuine, deck-the-halls, oh-come-all-ye-faithful holiday smash. It was also the beginning of a yuletide tradition, right?

Not so fast. Hard times kept on for Willam and Harold. In the years that followed, they couldn't always put on a holiday show. Meanwhile, Lew returned to New York from the war, but years in the army had done a number on his body. He couldn't dance like he'd danced before.

Still, Willam believed in his little brother. So did Harold.
And they believed he could help the San Francisco Ballet as a
choreographer and teacher. Come to California, they urged him.

By the next time Willam
and Harold staged *The
Nutcracker*—Christmas
1949—Lew was there.

The December after that, all three of them—Mr. C, Mr. Christensen, and Lew, as their dancers called them—put on *The Nutcracker* together. It was the right way to reunite, with three brothers doing what they loved. It was the right way to celebrate, with their holiday smash growing more smashing each year.

And it got a tradition going that continues today. Each December, you'll find *The Nutcracker* in San Francisco, New York, and all points in between.

To think that we have a trio of small-town
Utah boys to thank for that . . .

WHO WOULD'VE THOUGHT?

Author's Note

If you came to this book already knowing *The Nutcracker* or loving ballet, I'm so glad that I've been able to share with you this significant piece of history—a piece that, I'm betting, was unfamiliar to you.

But if you don't have much background in either one, I'm even happier that you're here, because that means you're willing to give new things a try. It also means that you're a lot like me.

I first heard of dance pioneers Willam, Harold, and Lew Christensen when Willam died in 2001. Before I read his obituary, I'd never given much thought to ballet. I did know, however, about *The Nutcracker,* and I could see that there was a story to tell: the Christensen brothers' role in a tradition that gets hundreds of thousands of Americans to the ballet each December.

In telling that story, I benefited greatly from the groundwork laid by Debra Hickenlooper Sowell in her 1998 academic biography *The Christensen Brothers: An American Dance Epic.* The interviews she conducted with Willam and Harold (Lew had already died when she began working on her book) and with dancers who worked with them are on file at the Museum of Performance + Design (MP+D) in San Francisco and were a huge help to me.

When I visited the MP+D in November 2013, the staff was generous with its time and assistance in supplying me not only with interview transcripts but also with other materials relating to the 1944 and 1949 productions of *The Nutcracker.* I am so grateful for the existence of such institutions and for all who help sustain them.

While I was in San Francisco, I also got to have lunch with the charming and gracious Nancy Johnson Poulos, who studied with the Christensens and appeared in both of those first productions during her formative years as a dancer. A few weeks later, my family took in a vibrant performance of *The Nutcracker* in our hometown of Austin, Texas. All the while, my efforts were guided by Millbrook Press's Carol Hinz, whose skill as an editor—paired with her own experience as a ballet dancer—deserves considerable credit for the book you've just read.

The lesson from all of this, for you and me alike, is to have confidence in our ability to explore new fields of study and to have faith that we will find people who can help guide us along. This was just as true for Willam, Harold, and Lew Christensen who—before any of them had heard of *The Nutcracker* or even done a single pirouette—were small-town boys who didn't know the first thing about ballet.

I'd say they did a pretty good job of figuring things out, wouldn't you?

Chris Barton

ILLUSTRATOR'S NOTE

I can't remember a time when I didn't want to draw and paint. I grew up in a big, messy, happy family, and my sisters received music and ballet lessons and my brother participated in wrestling and debate. I was lucky enough to take painting classes, and those classes sparked a passion that has stayed with me ever since.

When Carol Hinz contacted me about illustrating a book about *The Nutcracker*, my first thought—besides "YES!"—was, "Wow, me? Ballet?" I didn't know a plié from a passé.

Nonetheless, I kept thinking about the artist Edgar Degas and all those beautiful, graceful dancers he'd painted and sculpted. And the more I thought, the more excited I became. So I got to work. First up was to dig in and learn as much as I could about this thing called ballet.

Chris Barton very helpfully made his reading list available to me. I pored over each and every document looking for visual clues. What costumes did the dancers wear in those earlier productions? How did they style their hair? What did those brothers look like? I broadened my search, looking at hundreds of pictures of ballet dancers and watching more than a few *Nutcracker* videos on YouTube. I talked to everyone I knew who knew ballet.

I was finally comfortable enough to put pencil to paper. Rough sketches were placed in the layout alongside Chris's words. Both Carol and the book's art director, Danielle Carnito, had experience as ballet dancers. They checked and double-checked positions from fingertip to pointed toe and added to my growing knowledge.

Finally, I started creating the final art. My paintings begin with pencil on gesso, a white base layer. Then thin oil glazes are applied, one over another—as many as ten to fifteen glazes per painting. The process is slow and meticulous, but the resulting rich color intensity is worth the time and effort. For months I painted almost nonstop—engrossed in my work, dreaming about dance.

I have learned so much this past year, and although you will never find me in a pair of pointe shoes, I now count myself as a lover of ballet and truly admire the men and the women whose passion for what they do brings us this amazing art form.

CATHY GENDRON

TIMELINE

1816: German author E. T. A. Hoffmann writes a short story called *The Nutcracker and the Mouse King.*

1850s: The Christensen brothers' dance-loving, violin-playing grandfather, Lars Christian Christensen, immigrates to the United States from Denmark. He and his family settle in the Territory of Utah, as do the brothers' other grandparents.

A Nutcracker *performance in St. Petersburg, Russia, 1892*

1892: The ballet *The Nutcracker*—based on Hoffmann's story, with choreography by Marius Petipa and Lev Ivanov and music composed by Peter Ilyich Tchaikovsky—is performed for the first time at the Mariinsky Theatre in St. Petersburg, Russia. It does not catch on.

1902: William Christensen is born in Brigham City, Utah. He is the second child (following older brother Guy) of Christian and Isabell Farr Christensen. Brothers Harold and Lewellyn follow in 1904 and 1909.

1919: A new production of *The Nutcracker* by Moscow's Bolshoi Ballet is better received than the original version.

CA. 1920: William and Lew begin ballet training.

1925: Harold fails out of the United States Military Academy at West Point, New York, after one year. He returns to Utah and then starts learning ballet from William.

From the top: *Guy, William, Harold, and Lew Christensen, ca. 1911–1914*

1926: Leopold Stokowski conducts the Philadelphia Orchestra in a popular recording of Tchaikovsky pieces known as the *Nutcracker Suite.*

1927: William and Lew leave Utah. They debut on the vaudeville circuit with their revved-up, ballet-based act, Le Crist Revue. The act, later known as the Berkoffs and then the Mascagno Four before

Leopold Stokowski, ca. 1930

taking the name Christensen
Brothers and Company, settles in
New York City between tours.

1930: Harold moves to New
York to study ballet. Two years
later, William moves to Portland,
Oregon, and Harold takes his
place in the vaudeville act.

1934: William's ballet students
in Portland perform selections
from *The Nutcracker* at the city's
annual Rose Festival.

William (left) *and Lew* (right)
*Christensen with other vaudeville
dancers in 1926*

1935: Harold and Lew perform
their vaudeville act for the last
time. They decide to focus strictly on ballet and join New York's
Metropolitan Opera Ballet under Russian-born master George
Balanchine.

1938: As part of the Ballet Caravan organized by Lincoln
Kirstein, *Filling Station*—created by and starring Lew, and
also featuring Harold—makes its debut. Meanwhile, William
becomes head of the ballet company in San Francisco—and
begins using "Willam" as his professional name. (Friends and
family call him Bill.)

1940: Selections from the *Nutcracker Suite* are included in the
popular Walt Disney movie *Fantasia.* Harold begins teaching
ballet with Willam in San Francisco.

*Lew Christensen as Mac
in* Filling Station, *1938*

1942: Lew is inducted into the US Army. He serves in Europe until 1946.

1944: On Christmas Eve, the San Francisco Ballet puts on the first full-length American
production of *The Nutcracker,* choreographed by Willam and with dancers taught by Harold.

1949: With Lew on board as associate director, the San Francisco Ballet presents *The
Nutcracker* for a second time, establishing an annual holiday tradition.

1951: As Willam settles into a new role with the University of Utah in Salt Lake City,
he takes time away to choreograph a revised production of *The Nutcracker* with Lew in
San Francisco.

1954: Balanchine introduces his own version of *The Nutcracker* with the New York City Ballet.

1955: Willam brings the *Nutcracker* tradition home to Utah with performances by the University Theatre Ballet.

From left to right: *Harold, Willam, and Lew Christensen, ca. 1950*

1957: The New York City Ballet's staging of *The Nutcracker* reaches millions of homes when it is broadcast live on national television on Christmas night.

1963: In Salt Lake City, Willam establishes the Utah Civic Ballet, later known as Ballet West.

1984: Lew dies at the age of seventy-five, after thirty-three years as the director of the San Francisco Ballet.

1989: Fourteen years after retiring as director of the San Francisco Ballet School, Harold dies at the age of eighty-four.

2001: Willam dies at ninety-nine, just a few years after teaching his last class for Ballet West and just a few months after attending a performance of one of his ballets, where he received one last standing ovation.

THIS DECEMBER: Across the United States, there will be hundreds of productions of *The Nutcracker*—not just ballets but also versions featuring hip-hop, puppets, acrobats, you name it. Attendees who have read this book will know how that got started.

The Urban Ballet Theater blended elements of hip-hop, ballet, and other dance styles in its 2010 production of Nutcracker in the Lower.

The Whole Shebang, in a Nutshell: A Summary of *The Nutcracker*

One of the most fun things about attending a production of *The Nutcracker* is seeing how its costumes and plot and dances and design differ from those of other stagings— there's lots of room for creativity and interpretation within the basic story.

But what *is* the basic story?

Usually, it goes something like this: At a holiday party, a girl named Clara (but sometimes Marie) receives a wooden nutcracker doll from Drosselmeyer, a mysterious yet beloved guest. Her rambunctious brother, Fritz, breaks the doll, and Clara is distraught. That night, she dreams that she has shrunk down to the size of the mended nutcracker, who meanwhile has transformed into a rat-battling prince. Together, Clara and the Nutcracker Prince travel through the snow to the Land of Sweets, where they tell the ruling Sugar Plum Fairy the story of their journey thus far. In their honor, the Sugar Plum Fairy hosts a celebration featuring a dazzling variety of dances. Afterwards, Clara returns home with memories of her adventures to cherish along with Drosselmeyer's gift, which she will presumably keep out of Fritz's reach from now on.

Suggestions for Further Reading

Celenza, Anna Harwell. *Duke Ellington's Nutcracker Suite*. Illustrated by Don Tate. Watertown, MA: Charlesbridge, 2011.

Greenberg, Jan, and Sandra Jordan. *Ballet for Martha: Making Appalachian Spring*. Illustrated by Brian Floca. New York: Roaring Brook, 2010.

Hoffmann, E. T. A. *Nutcracker*. Illustrated by Maurice Sendak. New York: Crown, 1984.

Lee, Laura. *A Child's Introduction to Ballet: The Stories, Music, and Magic of Classical Dance*. Illustrated by Meredith Hamilton. New York: Black Dog & Leventhal, 2007.

Phelan, Matt. *Bluffton*. Somerville, MA: Candlewick, 2013.

Schubert, Leda. *Ballet of the Elephants*. Illustrated by Robert Andrew Parker. New York: Roaring Brook, 2006.

Stringer, Lauren. *When Stravinsky Met Nijinsky: Two Artists, Their Ballet, and One Extraordinary Riot*. Boston: Harcourt Children's Books, 2013.

Yolen, Jane, and Heidi E. Y. Stemple. *The Barefoot Book of Ballet Stories*. Illustrated by Rebecca Guay-Mitchell. Cambridge, MA: Barefoot Books, 2004.